JUMPSTART
YOUR
PLATFORM

....

A BEGINNERS GUIDE TO FIND-ING YOUR AUDIENCE THROUGH SOCIAL MEDIA

BY SCOTT LA COUNTE

BuzzTrace Publications
www.BuzzTrace.com

ANAHEIM, CALIFORNIA

Table of Contents

ABOUT BUZZTRACE PUBLICATIONS

BuzzTrace Publications is the publishing arm of BuzzTrace.com—online software to help writers and other content creators build, maintain and protect their platform. If you'd like to create a free account and grow your online presence, go to BuzzTrace.com.

INTRODUCTION

....

WHAT IS PLATFORM ANYWAY?

P latform. It can make or break a writer. If you have it, then get ready for publishers to offer you contracts; and if you don't? Let me kindly introduce you to the slush pile.

Whether you are a writer or another kind of content provider, there is one universal truth: you need platform. Most writers put all their effort into writing their book and haven't thought at all about their platform. In fact if you asked most new writers what their platform is, they will probably reply with a blank stare and a follow up question: what's platform?

If that person is you and you're sitting here reading and won-dering what platform is...platform is your message and the people who will buy your message. This book is geared at authors, but platform and how to build it is the same no matter who you are— be it a musician, a business, or a motivational speaker.

Publishers want to know you're an author who already has a proven market and they won't have to work hard to sell your book

—they want low risk with high return. So when they ask what your platform is, what they really want to know is what your message is and how many people are already buying into that message. Think of yourself on a stage with a podium and a mic—your platform is the message you are delivering to all the people in front of you; the bigger the audience the bigger your platform is.

When I sold my first book, *Quiet, Please: Dispatches From a Public Librarian*, I had no problem at all finding an agent; I sent query letters to six agents and didn't get a single rejection; that book started as a series of blogs for McSweeneys.net, and, it turned out, I had established a platform without even knowing it. This is rare in the publishing industry.

I got lucky. But instead of taking my luck and building off it, I went back to writing and figured I was a published writer now, so it would all be easy.

I was wrong, of course, and when it came time to sell my next book, agents and publishers weren't as eager to hear from me. The few that would lend me their ear always wanted to know one thing: what's your platform.

Many authors have tossed up their hands and decided to go the self-publishing route, only to discover that platform is important there as well. In fact it's more important. If you are traditionally published, you at least have someone holding your hand and helping you through the book promotion process. But if you are self-publishing, then this is all on you. How will people find this great book you've written if they don't know who you are?

So how do you build platform? In part one, I'll be looking at the three places most people start: blogs, Facebook, and Twitter. Part two gives a brief overview of how other social networks work; these include Google+, LinkedIn, Instagram, Goodreads, and Reddit.

PART ONE:

THE CRASH COURSE

TWITTER

....

A BEGINNERS GUIDE TO
FINDING YOUR FOLLOWERS

At its core, Twitter should be the easiest of the three social platforms I'll cover in this book. You only have to think of 140 characters to say—that's only one or two sentences. The mistake most people make when building their platform is they open a Twitter account and figure they can say anything and people will not only follow them, but buy their book or whatever product they are trying to sell. When nothing happens after a few weeks, they give up.

If you don't already have a Twitter account, then pay careful attention to the profile name you create. Keep it simple. No clever nicknames or book titles. Maybe you are all about the book you are writing now, but platform is about the long term—so naming your profile after your book will only help that book. You should be the platform: not your book. If the name is already taken, try adding author or writer to it. @johndoeauthor or @authorjohndoe for example.

The first thing you should remember is Twitter is a conversation. Some people may use it to spew off crazy thoughts, but most people who successfully grow their platform, do so by interacting with other people. Use Twitter to find your audience and learn about their likes and dislikes.

Before you think too hard about what you'll say, consider who you'll say it to. You don't start Twitter with followers, after all. So where do you find them? Start by following people you actually follow. Don't follow 5,000 people just so they'll maybe follow you back. Follow people you genuinely want to interact with—and people who would actually interact with you. You could follow Bill Clinton because you happen to like what he says, for example—but don't expect him to interact with you. Once you are following them, show you have interest in what they're saying by responding to their tweets and engaging in conversations.

Joining Twitter groups is a great place to find followers, but the same rules apply: if you are only joining a group to get followers, then you aren't going to get followers. Join groups you are interested in and want to interact with.

There's a number of websites to help connect you with people you have common interests with. Two popular ones to start with: http://twiends.com/ and followerwonk.com

Before tweeting something, ask yourself if someone would actually care: will it benefit them in anyway. Nobody will care that you had a tuna sandwich for lunch, unless you could make that sandwich a little more interesting...taking a picture of the sandwich, for instance, and then giving a recipe that shows why this sandwich is truly unique.

You're a writer, so you probably know all about your writing voice. That voice should carry over to social media as well; don't post uninspired tweets—show that you really are enjoying doing this and you aren't doing it because someone is twisting your arm.

When you first start out and you don't have a lot of followers, inspirational quotes are always a smart choice—they're commonly liked and retweeted by others.

Sharing interesting articles is another popular thing you can Tweet for engagement. But try and think of articles people may not actually have heard of. Don't tweet an article about who won the presidential race...tweet an article about something a little smaller, but that needs to be read.

Hashtags are one of the easiest ways to get followers quick...if you use them right. On Twitter, a hashtag is something that starts with a # sign...when a person clicks on the word after it, they see other people talking about that topic. So, for example, if you are talking about politics you might end your tweet with #politics.

Here's a few things to remember about hashtags. First: don't hashtag everything. Use them when they seem relevant, but every tweet doesn't need nor should it have a hashtag. Second: don't be generic; posting a tweet about how happy you are about something with #excited will not find you any followers. Third: use hashtags relevant to your followers—if you are at a writers conference, for example, and there's a hashtag for that conference: use it. This will connect you with other people at that same conference. The same is true with hashtags that are just for writers—#amwriting or #writerslife, for example, are two hashtags that are commonly used by other writers. Last, think of hashtags that build into your brand—unique hashtags that only you use. So, for example, you might have a hashtag for the book you are working on, and when-ever a reader clicks on it, they can see all the tweets about that particular book; or you may ask your readers to use a certain hash-tag whenever they talk about your book.

As you grow and start to get followers, start thinking about ways to make them get engaged with your Tweets. Charities are one place to start. Who doesn't want to help people? But instead of saying "Here's a great charity that helps kids read" say "Millions of kids can't read. Here's a charity that helps. Please retweet." In the second example you're asking your readers to actually respond to what your saying.

As an author you'll obviously want to make your tweets somewhat book inspired. You can do this by posting book recommendations or asking people what's on their reading list. But you can also occasionally promote other authors. Helping other writers will help yourself in the long term.

Finally, now that you have a Twitter account, don't forget to promote it everywhere you have presence—your business cards, your website, at the start of your book. On your website, feed your tweets directly into it, so new tweets show up on your website. Not only does this promote your Twitter account, but it makes it look like your website is updated.

One common mistake I hear from a lot of authors is "I just post on one place and it goes everywhere." Don't do that! We'll look at other social networks next, but always remember that your message on each network should change—people who regularly use Twitter are a different audience than people who use Face-book...so your message needs to be altered.

You may hear there's a secret sauce—an equation to go from 0 followers to millions overnight. But there's not. Anyone can have millions of followers...if they devote the time to build it. The question will quickly become not how large you want your platform to be, but how much time can you devote to building it.

FACEBOOK

....

A BEGINNERS GUIDE TO TELLING YOUR STORY

Y ou probably know some of the story of Facebook—how it

started in the dorm of a kid barely out of college as a way to connect other college kids together. Today it's used by billions of people all around the world. You use it to connect to friends, but also
to connect to your favorite brands.

That last bit: brands—that's something that wasn't introduced
until several years after Facebook started. That's what I'll be talking about in this chapter. How do you use this multi-billion user
base to grow your platform?

I use the word "brand" purposely because where Twitter is
more of a conversation, Facebook is more of a story. Twitter is
more informal—Facebook is really where you as a brand begin to
take shape and have a distinct tone.

Before I get too deep into what your Facebook strategy should
be, let me quickly state the obvious: your Facebook fan page
should be different from your Facebook personal page. Getting a

fan page is simple—you don't even need a separate account; you can manage it within your personal page. If you don't have one already, open up your personal Facebook page on your web browser (and these directions assume you aren't using a mobile device...it will be a little different if you are). Now look on the left side; about half way down under pages, there's an option that says CREATE and under it Ad, Page, Group, Event, Fundraiser. Click "Page"

Next click Create a Page, and select Artist, Brand or Public Figure.

Artist, Band or Public Figure

You can now select the category you fall under—such as blogger or writer, then add your name—remember this is the name your fans know you by, so if you have a pen name, then use that.

On the last page you can add your about section, picture and other relevant information.

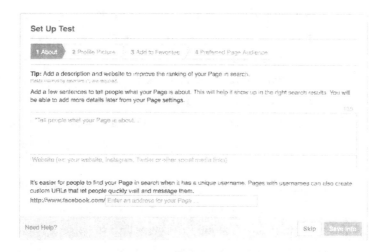

Once your page is ready, the first thing you should do is invite all of your personal Facebook friends; these will be your first real evangelists.

In the last section, I reminded readers not to share content across all networks. Let me warn you again. I know it's tempting to post the same content across all of your social networks. It's incredibly easy to do and it saves you time. And it lets all your fans see your content—you wouldn't after all want someone on Facebook to miss out simply because they don't have a Twitter account, right? Wrong! Let me say it again to make sure you understand: Wrong! Wrong! Wrong! Just don't do it! If one of your followers is absolutely furious that they missed out on something that you posted on Twitter but not Facebook, gently remind them that Twitter and Facebook are both free!

Posting separate content on both platforms encourages your fan base to follow you on both places; you have the potential to send your messages to them twice, so why not do it? What's more—what if the whole cross post thing backfires and people see the move as just plain lazy?

It's not the unforgivable sin to share occasional content across all platforms—but keep it to a minimum.

To help you understand why you should post the same content, it might be helpful to explain how Facebook and Twitter are different.

People tend to spend less time on Twitter than Facebook. That doesn't mean Facebook is more important because when you look at the demographics, people on Twitter tend to be younger, college educated and earn more money. They're a completely different group of people, so of course you'll want to have a different tone when engaging with them.

Facebook is more about engagement—use Twitter to talk to your fans—it's engagement, but it tends to be more informal engagement; use Facebook to engage with them—create content they'll absolutely want to share and like.

Twitter is in real-time. What do I mean by that? Twitter tends to be about what's going on in the day—it's very casual. You may talk about what you're writing or getting ready for. Your fans tend to see you in a much more personal and intimate way. Time usually doesn't matter Facebook—if someone reads it today or next week it wouldn't really matter.

I'll talk more about pay-to-play later, but if you are looking to grow your platform without spending money, you'll have an easier time on Twitter. Facebook makes you pay to boost your content— that means when you post something on Facebook and don't pay, then many of your fans will never see it.

Facebook is much, much more visual. Think about your own Facebook feed—what usually gets you to stop? Pictures! Even if you are posting a narrative on Facebook, you should always post a picture to go with it. You can post your own photo, buy stock photos, or use public domain photos. If you don't want to take your own photos or buy stock photos, then one website to check out is PublicDomainPictures.net. If you ever need free clipart, another website to bookmark is OpenClipart.org.

Pictures aside, what you need to establish very early on is your tone. Is this space going to be a place to post links? Announcements? Contests? When your readers think about your page, what do they think? Oh, that's the writer with the funny pictures? Insightful messages? Lively news? Think about who your readers will be and what they'll respond to. If you're a true crime writer your message will be much different then a romance writer. You can have all of the things I just mentioned, but everything needs to have a consistent tone.

Most successful fan pages have a schedule. Maybe every Friday is a funny graphic; every Monday is a story about being a writer. Schedules help keep you consistent, but also give your readers something to look forward to.

Recently Facebook began to let people search by hashtags. Most studies have shown hashtags on Facebook don't have quite the same effect on Facebook that they have on Twitter. That said, there's nothing that says it's a bad thing and it can still work in your favor...when done correctly. Just like Twitter, hashtags should not be overused. Use them when they're relevant to your post, and only use one or two of them. If you don't know what hashtag to use, http://Hashtagify.me is one popular website that helps you see what's trending. One reason hashtags could work in your favor is that it gives you a way to pull all of your social networks together—ask your fans to use the same hashtag wherever they may follow you.

Just like Twitter, you want to make sure links to your Facebook page are everywhere you are. You need to make sure it's as easy as humanly possible for your fans to find you on Facebook. So have that link on your website, your email, your LinkedIn profile—everywhere.

One last thing you need to know about: pay-to-play. While it's possible to grow your fan page without paying a dime, if you are hoping to grow your platform quickly, then be prepared to open your wallet. Unfortunately, Facebook is making it more and more difficult to have an organic reach with your readers. That means when you share content, many of your fans won't even see it in their news feed—or it will be so far buried, it will be lost to them.

Whenever you post something, there's an option to boost the post. Boosting the post means you pay to get people see it. Personally, I think it's worth a small investment to experiment with it. Start with $10 and see what you think.

The advantage of the boost is that you can send your message to people who don't even follow you. If they like that message, then you can send an invite to them to like your fan page. So, for instance, you may boost something for $50 and get 60 people to like your page. The important thing to remember is that this is something you do for your absolute best content. If you're paying for it, then get the best bang for your buck.

You can also target the boost. So, for example, let's say you're speaking to woman's group in Dallas and the audience will be mostly women in their 30s. You can announce your speaking engagement and set it up so only women in their 30s who live in the Dallas area see it.

It can be discouraging to hear you have to pay for fans, but remind yourself that these may be the people who will later pay you for your book.

If all of this sounds like a lot of work, then you are hopefully starting to understand platform. Building your platform is a job. I hope writing is something you enjoy, but at the end of the day, if you are going to be successful at it, then you have to start viewing it not as a hobby, but as a job.

Most people don't have the time or money to quit their day jobs to devote all their time to writing and building their platform. But you really don't have to. Devoting just an hour a day to your platform will put you on your way to huge growth. It will probably take time, but don't give up and it will happen.

21

So in the last section I talked about creating content at its absolute shortest: Twitter. In this section we saw how to start giving your message more of a story; in the next section we'll see the final piece of the puzzle: blogs.

BLOGGING

....

DO PEOPLE STILL READ BLOGS?

Octpber 22, 1997. To most people this date is of little im-
portance. Why does it matter? This is the day that Open Diary
launched. Open Diary is often cited as the first blog that allowed
users to comment; it's often cited as one of the first real modern
examples of the blog. Before it, there had been forms of blogs in
existence, but this was one of the best examples of the blogs we'd
come to know today.

The idea of Open Diary was to let users from around the
world share their diary online. Millions of diaries were written.
The website was huge, and one of the first success stories of the
blogging age.

23

Where is Open Diary today? You can still go to OpenDiary.-com and see an archive of it. Why an archive? Because it doesn't exist anymore. Open Diary stopped in 2014.

What happened? How did a website go from huge to gone? If we're going to point fingers, the best place to start is our attention spans. As the Internet aged, the attention span of Internet users got lower—soon people moved from blogs to tweets; and when even a tweet was too much work, they moved on to pictures. When we think of platform today, many will not even turn to blogs—or they'll look at them as a mere footnote.

Blogging was great when that was all we had...but now we can cram blogs into tweets or even pictures. We can save time and do things that really matter—like searching for videos of the monkey cowboy rodeo. Go ahead and stop reading for a moment to check that out—I know you're tempted!

So all of this begs the important question: do blogs matter?

The answer to that question is yes...but only if you use them right. As you're probably starting to see if you've read the other two sections, your social media presence matters when you make it matter. Do it right and you're on your way to a large following; do it wrong and you'll only be disappointed.

If you're new to writing, one of the biggest reasons you should blog is because it gets you to write. You need the discipline. Challenge yourself to set blogging goals. As you blog more something else will happen: you get better as a writer.

What should you write about? Before you ask that, you should ask who you are writing for. Just as Facebook and Twitter have a tone, your blog should obviously have one too.

Once your blog is written, it doesn't hurt to post it on Medium.com as well to give it extra exposure and find more readers.

In its heyday, bloggers would find their audience by getting to know other bloggers and guest blogging. That still happens today, but not to the same extent. Today one of the easiest ways to get exposure is to link it back to your other social media accounts. When you write a blog, post a link to it on Facebook and Twitter— funnel your other channels into it.

Most importantly, write blogs that matter. What topics will people click on when you post links across your social networks? One thing that remains important to blogs is good SEO; a blog with the right keywords can ultimately drive people from Google to your website.

Don't be afraid to be you. Blogs are the best way to show your voice to your readers; it can be a place to post added content that perhaps you weren't able to get in a book. Or just an avenue to talk about something you want to talk about; blogs, at their core, are ultimately an online diary—a place for authors to be more un-censored.

If you're stuck, here are arguably the best topics to blog about —write about them and you'll almost certainly get good traffic:

- List—these can be anything from gift guides to history (such as, 10 world leaders who really sucked)
- How-to's—everyone is an expert at something...here's your chance to show off to the world.
- Essential guides (such as essential guide to being a bestselling author)
- Frequently asked questions that you get
- Interviews—if you can get a celebrity, all power to you— but interviews can also be with interesting people...people who have interesting jobs, doing interesting things, or have weird hobbies.

One thing to remember about blogs is: you own the content. Sure anything you post on Twitter or Facebook you own—but it's hosted on someone else's domain. That means if the social network becomes the next MySpace, or worse, Friendster, there's not an easy way for your readers to go back and look at some of your older stuff.

One other reason to blog: you can make money from it. While you're working on your next book, you have all these little articles online. There's no rule that says you can't put all this content into a book of blogs and make money. There are rules that would prevent you from enrolling it in a program like KDP Select, however.

PART TWO:

GETTING SOCIAL

Note: This Content Has Been Excerpted With Permission from "A Newbies Guide to Social Networking" by Minute Help Guides

GOOGLE+

....

GOOGLE'S DESPERATE ATTEMPT TO BE FACEBOOK

Who Should Use It

Google+ is Google's popular new social networking platform designed to rival many of the other social networking sites available today, while seamlessly integrating with your Google identity. It replicates and improves upon many of the features of social networking powerhouses like Facebook, Flickr, and even Skype. It attempts to improve upon other social networking sites by enhancing privacy settings through the use of "circles," allowing users to granularly select which groups of people to share different information with. Through the use of circles, you might be able to share your latest escapades at the dance club only with people in your Friends circle, and choose not to share that information with people in your coworkers or family circles. Google+ can also manage photosets (much like Flickr or Facebook) and allow for "Hangouts," or video chat between many different people.

If you're interested in sharing information about your life in text, photo and video form, and/or you're already a Google user, you'll probably want to see what Google+ has to offer.

Sign-Up Process

If you already have an account with Google (for Gmail or for the use of other Google services), signing up to use Google+ is as simple as visiting plus.google.com and logging in with your Google identity. If you don't yet have an account with Google, it's not a bad idea to go ahead and create one, whether or not you intend to stick with Google+.

To sign up for a Google account, click the sign up link on the plus.google.com website, and fill out the information requested. You can skip the mobile phone field if you'd like, but entering your mobile phone will help if you ever need to verify your account or reset your password.

Finding People to Follow in Google+

Clicking on any of these categories will automatically create a new circle for you with the name of that category and containing the people or groups listed along with it.

Finally, you'll be asked to provide a photo and some information about yourself such as where you work or go to school and where you live. This information is optional, but can help people to find you on Google+

After completing that information, you'll be taken to your Google+ page where you can start using the service right away.

Crash Course in Google+

After signing in to Google+, you'll be taken to your Home screen. If you've used Facebook before, this should look very similar to your Facebook newsfeed, with posts from people you "follow" (in Google+ these are the people you've added to your Circles) presented in the middle. On any of the posts in your Google+ newsfeed, you can click the +1 symbol to show your support for the post (or, in Facebook terms, "like" the post). Anyone who can see the original post can see your +1. You can see who can view the original post on the top line (in the example below, the post is public). You can also reshare the post on your own profile by clicking the arrow symbol next to the +1. You can also see how many people have +1'ed or reshared the post at the bottom right.

Like Facebook, users can comment on posts in their newsfeed.

Circles

Before you begin sharing on Google+, it's important to understand what Circles are and how to use them. Click the Circles icon on the left of the screen to view your circles.

Circles in Google+

By default, Google+ gives you four circles: Friends, Family, Acquaintances, and Following. You can also add new circles as needed—for example, coworkers or Tuesday Night Poker Buddies. As you establish contacts in Google+, you can organize them into circles to help you keep everyone straight. By using circles, you can customize exactly who sees what you share on Google+.

For example, you might share photos of your new car with your Friends and Family circles, a work tip with your coworkers circle, and your winnings from your most recent poker tournament with your Tuesday Night Poker Buddies circle. The Following circle can be used for people whose posts you'd like to see, but who you don't necessarily want seeing your own posts (like public figures or famous people).

From the Circles page, you can drag any contact into a circle to quickly add that person to the circle, and you can delete people from your circles as necessary.

Sharing

Now that you've set up Circles, it's easy to start sharing. From your home screen in Google+, there is an area at the top with a text box that you can use to share whatever information you want. You can type text in the text bar, or drag most types of multimedia files or links into the box to share anything from pictures and videos to links to YouTube videos.

After typing in or adding the content you want to share, you'll have to specify with whom to share your post. You can choose individual contacts that you might have in Google+, individual or multiple circles that you've set up, and even individual email addresses if you'd like to share with someone who does not yet use Google+. You can choose to make your share public, or to just share the post with people in all of your circles.

It's important to note that just because someone is in a circle you are sharing with, the person doesn't necessarily follow you back and might not see everything you share with that circle.

Sharing Photos

For a long time, Google's Picasa website and application was one of Flickr's biggest competitors in terms of photo organization and sharing. With the advent of Google+, Picasa has been integrated into Google+ and is now simply called Photos. To begin seeing the features contained with Photos, click the Photos icon on the left side of the screen.

There are a few ways to add photos to Google+. Anytime you share a photo in one of your posts, it will be added to the "From Posts" category in the Photo section. Any circles or individuals you specified in the original post will be able to see this photo.

If you use the Google+ app for iPhone or Android devices, you can share photos instantly from your phone to Google+ and similarly specify with which circles or individuals to share the photos.

Anytime someone tags a photo of you on Google+, it will be automatically added to the Photos of You category on the Photos page. Anyone in a circle that was included when the post was originally shared can see this photo of you, but you may un-tag yourself at any time.

Clicking the Upload Photos button in the top right corner will allow you to upload photos in bulk to Google+ and will automatically organize each set of uploads into an album. Simply drag the photos you want to share into the box to begin the process.

After the photos upload, Google+ will automatically identify people in the photo and offer you a chance to tag those people. Over time, it will begin to learn (or at least make a reasonable guess at) different faces. It will even prompt you to try to find your face in other people's photos on Google+.

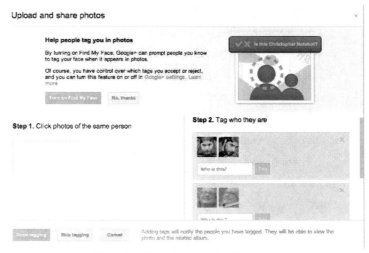

Find My Face Feature in Google+

When you are done tagging photos, you can add a comment to the album, and then choose who to share it with.

Hangouts

Another key part of Google+ is the Hangout feature. Hangout allows you to video chat with up to nine friends at the same time, which at the moment exceeds Skype's capabilities for video conferencing.

To start a hangout, click the "Hang Out" button on the right side of the screen. The first time you use this feature, you'll be prompted to install the Google Voice and Video Plugin. Just click the Install Plugin button and then follow the instructions on the screen.

Before you start the hangout, you can preview what others will see in the small video window below the form.

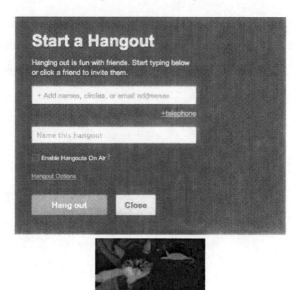

Starting a Google+ Hangout

After installing the plugin, you can then invite people to the hangout by inviting individual friends, entire circles, and non-Google+ users by email address. You can even invite landline and cell phone numbers to the hangout (this is a free service for calls to the US or Canada in 2012, but you can also call internationally at very low rates). You can then name the hang out, and even choose to record and broadcast the hangout live over YouTube if you want.

Editing your Profile

Click the Profile icon on the left part of the screen to edit your Google Profile. Like Facebook, you can fill out information such as place of employment, education, places you've lived, contact information, and relationship status. However, with the added benefit of circles, you can control specifically who is able to see each piece of information about you. In this area you can also control which photos you are tagged in and in what posts you appear.

LINKEDIN

....

DOES LINKEDIN WORK FOR MY PLATFORM?

Who Should Use It

Unlike most of the other networks discussed in this guide, LinkedIn is designed purely for professional networking – personal use is possible, but the main focus of the site is building an online presence in your career field or industry.

LinkedIn is an extremely useful tool for people looking to make and maintain professional contacts, whether they work for an organization or as a freelancer. If you are currently looking for work, your LinkedIn profile can serve as a powerful search result when your prospective employer (inevitably) performs a Google search for your name. LinkedIn is a chance to showcase your professional life, as well as a tool for controlling your online professional presence.

Sign-Up Process

Signing up for LinkedIn is simple. Visit www.linkedin.com and fill in the registration form you'll find on the very first page. You'll need to enter your real name, email address, and a password that you can easily remember. Then click "Join Now" to get started. Once you've registered for LinkedIn, you'll have the opportunity to create your LinkedIn profile. It's worth thinking about this step before you even register – on LinkedIn, you'll want to include (at a minimum) a current, professional photo, your work history, skills, education and experience. If you have a current resume handy, you'll find that creating your profile is much simpler!

Crash Course in LinkedIn

When you're starting out in LinkedIn, remember that this networking site is geared toward professionals – think of LinkedIn as an online portfolio or resume. You'll want to put your best foot forward on your profile, but remember that your contacts reflect on you as well! In this crash course, we'll cover your LinkedIn profile, managing and maximizing LinkedIn connections, searching for jobs, and the benefits of upgrading your LinkedIn account.

Your LinkedIn Profile
Your LinkedIn profile is the single most important aspect of LinkedIn. Take as much time with this as you would with a professional resume, and keep it up to date! To view or edit your profile, click the Profile link in the top menu bar.

Viewing and Editing Your Profile

There are several aspects of your profile that will appear as hyperlinks. The names of the organizations you've worked for or with, the skills and expertise you've listed, and educational institutions.

Profile Completeness

LinkedIn lets you know how you're doing with your profile by indicating its completeness as a percentage. Do everything you can to get your profile up to 100%!

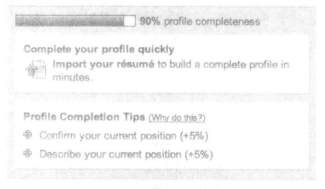

Profile Completeness Indicator

Profile Applications

One potentially confusing aspect of your LinkedIn profile can be found at the bottom of the profile editing page – applications. Now, on a job and career site, you would be forgiven for thinking that applications referred to actual job applications. But in LinkedIn, there are fifteen widget-like applications that can be added to your profile to further showcase your skills and experience. If you have a Wordpress blog, a Slideshare account, or GitHub projects you're working on, you can add applications to highlight them.

Connecting with LinkedIn

Your LinkedIn connections are the people you've worked with or know in a professional context. Your connections can open new doors for you by helping you find job opportunities or by writing recommendations for you. You'll want a robust connections list on your profile – not only does it demonstrate to anyone viewing your profile that you have a healthy professional support network, it also helps you reach out to your network effectively.

Searching for Connections

You can search for LinkedIn connections individually using the search box in the top right corner, or you can import connections from your email account. You can also find coworkers and former coworkers very easily after you've created your LinkedIn profile. Just click on the name of one of your employers to see a snapshot of the organization, including links to every employee or former employee currently registered on LinkedIn. This is also a useful strategy to help you prepare for job interviews, since you can get an idea of the faces behind the titles!

Like Facebook, in LinkedIn you send invitations to connect. It's up to the recipient to approve, deny or ignore the request.

Your LinkedIn Network

When you make a connection on LinkedIn, your new connection's connections become a part of your network. Your personal connection is a first degree connection, and their contacts are second degree connections for you. Second degree contacts' connections are third degree connections for you, and so on and so forth.

You'll notice your network growing exponentially as you add connections. This is a great way to discover links to key individuals that you may not have realized you were so closely connected to!

YOUR LINKEDIN NETWORK

68 Connections link you to 1,278,818+ professionals

1,900 New people in your Network since October 14

Network Stats in LinkedIn

InMail

InMail is LinkedIn's direct message feature, which allows you to contact LinkedIn members outside your own connections network. Unlike Facebook or Twitter, though, InMail isn't free. You'll have to either upgrade your account or purchase InMail in order to use it.

Find References

If you're viewing a profile and you'd like to find references for the person (for example, if you're looking to hire someone), use the menu pictured above and click Find References.

Connections Updates

LinkedIn shows you updates from your connections – who's connecting with who, who's updating their profile, who's received recommendations, etc.

There are a few social features available in your LinkedIn updates. You can like some updates, like endorsements, new jobs, and written updates. It's a nice gesture to use the "Say Congrats" feature if one of your connections moves into a new job!

You can share to LinkedIn if you like using the Share an Update text field. You can attach links and link the update to your Twitter feed by checking the box next to the Twitter bird icon.

Sharing Updates in LinkedIn

Again, though, remember that LinkedIn is meant for professional activity. Don't use LinkedIn updates for personal shares or anything you wouldn't want to say or endorse at work.

Recommendations and Endorsements

If you'd like to really shine on LinkedIn, it's a good idea to request recommendations from your key connections. LinkedIn makes this very simple with its form email feature. It gives you a subject and default text for the email, and you simply select which positions you'd like a recommendation for and who in your connections you'd like to send the request to. Don't be shy about this. It's no different from requesting a recommendation letter, and it gives your LinkedIn profile much more credibility.

Endorsements are similar to recommendations, but require less work! All you have to do to endorse someone is visit his or her profile, scroll down to the skills and experience list, and click the plus sign next to each skill you want to endorse. LinkedIn will also help you endorse skills by posting recommended endorsements at the top of your connections' profiles. You can even write in skills that the person left out. It's fast and easy and really helps improve a LinkedIn profile!

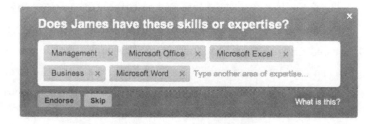

Recommended Endorsements

It's highly recommended to endorse members of your LinkedIn network, if you can do so in good conscience. It's a great way to strengthen a professional connection. It may also inspire your connections to return the favor!

....

BUILD YOUR PLATFORM ONE PICTURE AT A TIME

Who Should Use It

Instagram is a must-have free social platform for anyone who uses the camera on his or her phone. Unlike Facebook and many other social networks covered in this guide, Instagram can only be used as an app. Instagram for iPhone and Android allows you to easily take and share photos to people you follow on Instagram, or to your followers on Facebook, Tumblr, and Twitter. It also allows you to easily email photos you take on your phone to anyone in the world. You can use built in Filters to give your cell phone pictures a creative look. Instagram integrates with your photo albums on your phone so you can access them in other applications or send them to other peoples' phones by MMS.

In short, Instagram gives you a simple and powerful set of tools for sharing photos from your phone above and beyond your native camera app.

Sign-Up Process

Jumpstart Your Platform

Instagram is primarily managed from your phone or device that will be taking the photos, so the first step to getting signed up is to install the application on your phone. Simply search for it in the Apple App Store if you use an iPhone or iPad, or from Google Play if you use an Android device.

After the app is installed, you'll need to register a new Instagram account. Just tap the Sign Up button to get started.

You'll next need to provide some information to register your account. Fill out your desired username and password and (if desired) a profile picture. Alternately, you can provide your Facebook credentials to quickly sign up.

Instagram will keep your phone number and email address private at all times, and only those people you specify can see your activity on Instagram.

Crash Course in Instagram

After registering with Instagram, you can immediately start snapping, editing, and sharing your photos. To start taking photos, tap the middle camera icon.

In Instagram Camera Mode, the square icon on the top left will turn borders off and on for your photo. The lightning bolt icon will allow you turn your phone's flash off, on, or set it to fire automatically. The middle icon will allow you to use either the default camera or the front facing camera (if available). The water drop icon will apply a water drop effect where the center will appear in focus and the outer edges (or the vertical edges) will appear blurry. Press the X button to cancel taking a photo.

When you are ready to take a picture, press the bottom middle icon. If you'd rather share or edit a photo already on your camera, you can press the icon on the bottom right to choose which photo to use. If you want to choose a filter before snapping your picture, you can press the square icon with a triangle in the center (more on filters coming up).

Editing a Photo in Instagram

After taking a photo, you can apply one of a number of different filters that come with Instagram. Make sure to play with the filters to get the best look for your photo! Notice that you can still add a border or water drop effect at this point. Additionally, you can press the icon on the bottom left to increase the brightness and contrast of your shot. When you're satisfied with your photo, sim-ply press the green check mark to specify what you want to do with your photo next.

On the resulting screen, you can leave a comment about the picture, choose to add it to your Photo Map (more on the Photo Map in a minute), and then choose which services you'd like to share the photo to: Facebook, Twitter, Tumblr, Flickr, or Foursquare. Alternately, you can choose to email the photo, or if you choose none of these options, it will only be saved to your Instagram account and to the photo library on your phone. You can always share it later if you want!

Sharing an Instagram Photo

In order to share with web services like Facebook, Instagram will first require you to log into your account on the service's site (linked from Instagram), and then the website will require you to authorize Instagram to post on your behalf. It only takes a few seconds to authorize each web service, and then you can quickly and easily share directly to that service from the Instagram app.

After sharing on a web service like Facebook, any likes or comments you receive on Facebook (or other social networks) will translate over to Instagram and vice versa.

When you're done taking and sharing a photo, you will be returned to the home screen, which will show the photos you've taken and any comments or likes you've received from any web service.

You can use the buttons at the bottom of the screen to navigate to different parts of the Instagram service. The home button on the left will return you to your home screen where you can see all of your photos and their likes and comments. The second icon will take you to the Explore page, where you can search for specific users on Instagram or explore other users' tagged photos. For example, searching for "Hawaii" will return any photo that people have tagged with #hawaii.

Back on the Instagram menu, the middle icon returns you to the camera so that you can take more pictures, as previously discussed. The fourth icon, a heart in a speech bubble, will give you a timeline of activity on your photos. This will allow you to see, in chronological order, when people like or comment on your photos.

Finally, the fifth button will allow you to edit the information saved in your profile and manage your Instagram account. It will also allow you to turn your photo map on or off. Each photo you take is saved with its geographic location, and, if you turn that feature on (it is left off by default, for privacy reasons), each of your photos will be placed on a map. This is a great feature for anyone who does a lot of traveling and wants to share the experience with family and friends!

SCOTT LA COUNTE

GOODREADS

....

BOOKS CONNECTING PEOPLE

Who Should Use It

Goodreads is designed for readers – it's a social network based entirely on books. Use it to keep track of what you've read, what your friends have read, what you thought about your books, and to discover great new things to read.

Goodreads contains many features similar to other social networks, like direct messages, a news feed of your Goodreads contacts' updates, and liking and commenting features. However, everything in Goodreads is entirely geared toward finding great new books to read. It can be integrated with other social network accounts, but Goodreads users have one thing and one thing only on their minds – books!

Sign-Up Process

To sign up for Goodreads, just visit www.goodreads.com. You'll see the registration form on the very first page. It's a pretty easy one, too – just enter your name, an email address, and a password. Click Register to get started.

After you've signed in for the first time, you'll have the option to import contacts from Facebook, Twitter, or your email accounts. If you'd rather add friends individually, you can do so later – just click Skip this Step. Next, Goodreads will ask you what your favorite genres are – select some if you like, but don't feel like you need to box yourself in! From there, you're ready to start adding, rating and reviewing books. Read on to learn how!

Crash Course in Goodreads

Goodreads is for and by avid readers – think of it as your personal and eternal book discussion club. Like most social networks, Goodreads revolves around profiles, friends, and updates, but on Goodreads, each of the three is heavily tied to books and reading.

Adding Books to Goodreads

One of the first things you'll want to do when you get started with Goodreads is to add your favorite books (if you haven't already done so while registering). Adding books is easy, and Goodreads' catalog is extensive. You can search by title, author or ISBN, if you're feeling extremely specific. Use the white search box next to the Goodreads logo at the top of the page to search for an individual title. If you click the magnifying glass, you'll get a more advanced search interface (pictured below).

Searching for Books in Goodreads

If you can't find the book you want to add (unlikely), you can always manually add the title using the "Manually Add a Book" link in the top right of your search results. Goodreads will give you a form to add the book that would make librarians proud – however, please be careful not to add duplicates to the system!

You can also import books from a spreadsheet if you have one, or from a webpage where book listings include ISBN numbers (like an Amazon Wish List, for example).

Once you've added your books, they'll appear in your "My Books" screen, which you can always get to at the top of the page. To get great recommendations from your friends and from the Goodreads platform, try rating your books using Goodreads' five star rating system. If you've got more to say, leave a review! Your ratings and reviews will help other Goodreads users decide whether or not they're interested in the title.

In Goodreads, you can organize your books into "bookshelves." There are three default bookshelves in Goodreads – read, reading, and to-read. The to-read shelf is a great place to keep a running list of all those books you hope to read in the future, whereas the read and reading lists help you keep track of your book history and let your Goodreads contacts know what you're working on right now.

However, you can further organize your books by genre, time period, etc. by creating custom bookshelves. It's easy to do. Simply click the Add Shelf link in the left menu. Then, after your shelf is set up, visit your My Books page, find the title you want to add to the new shelf, and click Edit.

Friends in Goodreads

In Goodreads, your friends share what they're reading and how they feel about it. Much like Facebook, your Goodreads home screen shows a real-time newsfeed of your friends' activity – reviews and ratings, new titles added, etc. You can also send direct messages to your friends, recommend books, or write "stories" that detail how you know each other (stories must be verified by the other person before they are posted). Goodreads is a useful exploratory and cataloging feature on its own, but with friends, it becomes an ongoing book discussion that can be downright addictive.

Adding Friends

To add friends, click the Friends icon right next to your name in the top right corner. This will show you all of your current friends, and give you some options for adding new ones. You can import friends from your Gmail, Hotmail, Twitter, Facebook and Yahoo! accounts, or you can explore friends of your Goodreads friends.

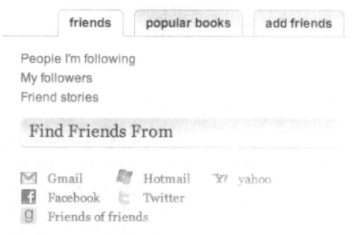

Adding Friends in Goodreads

If you want to add friends manually, click the "Add Friends" tab. This will give you a search box where you can search for your friend's name or email address. If they're already a Goodreads user, you can add them here, or if they haven't joined the site, you can send an invitation.

Compare Books

One of the most fun features on Goodreads is the Compare Books feature. This allows you to see how your literary tastes stack up against other Goodreads users. See how many books you and your friends have in common, and how similar your tastes are. The Compare Books link appears next to each friend on your friends list, as seen below.

Your Goodreads Profile

The Goodreads profile is fairly minimal; however, it will help your real-life friends find and recognize you on Goodreads, and it only takes a minute to fill out.

To edit your profile, click the downward arrow next to your profile picture (or the place holder image) in the top right corner. Fill out as much or as little as you'd like, and add a profile picture. You can tell Goodreads whether or not to display your last name, and several other fields have privacy settings built right in to the profile form.

Linking Accounts

You can link Goodreads to Facebook and Twitter to share your reviews and ratings with a much broader audience. To connect your accounts, visit your profile editing page and click on the Apps tab.

Goodreads will give you options for connecting to your Facebook, Twitter and Wordpress accounts, as well as instructions for installing the Goodreads mobile app on your phone.

Groups

Goodreads offers a number of groups based on common interests, genres, time periods and much more. There are reading groups that focus on a particular book, like *Moby Dick.* If you're not sure how to start making friends on Goodreads, try finding a group that piques your interest and go from there! Of course, if nothing looks good, you can always click "Create a Group" to start your own.

Tags

Tags in Goodreads have a personal and social function. You can use them as a personal taxonomy system for your own books, or you can use them to make your favorite books discoverable to other users. You can search for and browse other user's tags, which range from the general ("fiction") to the more specific ("vampires").

Exploring Books in Goodreads

Goodreads gives you several tools for finding something good to read. You can check out your friends' shelves or use the Explore and Recommendations menus to find books you may have never heard of that fit your interests. You can also peruse other Goodreads users' reviews under each title. You'll find that they tend to be thoughtful and detailed (reviews with spoilers are hidden as a courtesy). If a review helps you, be sure to "like" it!

Other Features in Goodreads

Goodreads contains a number of highly entertaining extra features that make an account worth any bookworm's while. Use the Explore menu at the top of the page to find extras like giveaways, trivia, quizzes and quotes. You'll also a link to Listopia here.

Goodreads' Listopia brings together crowd sourced lists in just about every genre, theme, and format. Listopia lists consist of titles that Goodreads users have voted for, making them more egalitarian than one or two reviewers' best-of lists found elsewhere online. Lists on Listopia can be browsed by genre or most popular. You can also check out featured lists. You can create your own list by using the Create a List link at the top, but it's up to the Goodreads community to decide which titles will go on it!

Finally, readers aren't the only ones who use Goodreads regularly. Authors (many of them quite famous) frequent the site as well, and you'll have access to exclusive interviews, debut author snapshots and more.

REDDIT

....

SOCIAL NEWS AGGREGATION

Who Should Use It

Reddit is a content aggregator, which means that users can submit links to content on the Internet that they find interesting. Other users of Reddit can then vote these links up or down, giving a good idea of what is popular at any given moment. Users can also comment on links that have been shared, and there is a very large and active community of commenters on the website. There are also "subreddits" that focus on individual categories, such as Technology, Movies, Politics, etc. so that users can quickly find trending topics in any field they might be interested in. Any user can create a subreddit on the topic of their choice, and can even make that subreddit private, making team collaboration for special projects easy!

Reddit is a great choice for anyone who wants to keep up to date with what's popular on the internet at any given time, and anyone who wants to share their favorite links with others.

Sign-Up Process

To sign up for Reddit, visit www.reddit.com and click the Register link in top right. From here, create a user name, enter your email address and password, and hit enter (or click Create Account). Reddit is somewhat cryptic as to whether or not this process is as easy as it appears – trust us, though, it is! You don't even need to enter an email address to register. Just choose a username and password, and you can get started right away!

The only tricky part of the sign-up process is finding a user name that hasn't already been taken. You'll probably have to settle for a user name other than your first choice. Fortunately, Reddit instantly checks your user name, so you'll only have to deal with the CAPTCHA (that string of letters that proves you're not a robot) once.

Anyone can view Reddit whether or not they have an account—simply visit reddit.com, and you'll have full access to viewing the links on the main page or within the subreddits (categories) listed along the top. However, if you'd like to be able to vote content up or down, or if you'd like to leave a comment, then you'll need to create an account.

Crash Course in Reddit

Reddit is an exciting and vibrant online community, but the text-heavy interface can feel a little overwhelming at first. This crash course will show you how to navigate Reddit, understand subreddits, submit to Reddit, and follow users and accrue karma. We'll also give you an introduction to Reddit etiquette, managing your preferences, and finding help.

Navigating Reddit

Reddit has been around since 2005, and has steadily grown in popularity since then. It calls itself "the front page of the internet," and in many ways it acts like a social newspaper digest for what's popular on the web based on user votes.

The "front page" (the page you land on when you visit reddit.com) in fact is a list of the most popular links shared recently on Reddit that might come from any category (called "subreddits") on Reddit. Much like the front page of a newspaper, this will list the most popular links from any subreddit based on overall user votes.

To view a shared link, simply click on the title. The domain that the link leads to is listed next to the link so you can have an idea of what domain you will visit before you click—the example below leads to a Tumblr page.

To view the comments that have been left on Reddit, click the text that lists the number of comments.

3073 ▓▓▓▓ submitted 5 hours ago by aertime
⬇   1008 comments share save hide report

top 200 comments show 500
sorted by: **best** ▾

(save)   formatting help

⬆ [-] yoyoltama 1481 points 2 hours ago
⬇ http://i.minus.com/ibvBaTD9OXHXu1.gif
I think that is a little bit better imo
permalink report reply

   ⬆ [-] viaGalactica 352 points 1 hour ago
   ⬇ As a redditor, this is better.
   permalink parent report reply

      ⬆ [-] Baelorn 9 points 53 minutes ago
      ⬇ **Relevant video:** http://www.youtube.com/watch?v=Veg63B8ofnQ
      permalink parent report reply

A Post on Reddit

Just like the links shared on Reddit, comments left on Reddit are sorted by votes given by other redditors, and so the highest voted comments are moved to the top of the thread. If you have created an account and logged in to Reddit, you can leave your own comment in the text box or reply to another user's comment.

If you'd like to tailor the types of links you're seeing, you can click on specific subreddits along the top of any page on the website. If you click on the "MORE" link on the right, you can subscribe and unsubscribe from any subreddit to better tailor your front page.

After you have created an account and logged in, you can vote links and any comment up or down. You can see the overall number of points (up-votes minus down-votes) a particular link or comment has received to get an idea of its popularity on Reddit.

Subreddits

There's a lot going on in Reddit, and if you're not sure where to get started, try exploring subreddits. We'll go through two of the most popular here, but don't be afraid to explore the subjects that interest you the most!

One of the most popular categories on Reddit is the IAmA subreddit. In this subreddit, an OP ("original poster") can create a post where he or she will answer questions from the Reddit community. Many famous people have held an AMA ("ask me anything") session—including President Barack Obama, Stephen Colbert, Ron Paul, and many others. President Obama's AMA was so popular that the high amount of traffic shut down the website at times!

The IAmA subreddit isn't limited to famous people; many people with interesting jobs, who live in strange places, or even people who might have some sort of specialized knowledge can create an IAmA post. For example, at the time of writing, one of the top IAmA threads of the day is "I am a cardiac surgeon, part of my job is to harvest hearts from living organ donors. AMA."

Another popular category on Reddit is the "TODAY-ILEARNED" (TIL) subreddit. In this category, users can post any piece of trivia that they might have learned that day. There are very strict rules for ensuring that all posts are verifiable and accurate, and opinion free. Visit this subreddit – you just might learn something!

There are new subreddits created every day and they range from general topics like Politics and Gaming to topics as specific as My Little Pony and Minecraft. Check them out or create your own!

Submitting to Reddit

After you've gotten your feet wet with the site, you can start to submit your own content to Reddit. Simply click the "Submit a link" button on the right side of every page.

You will be taken to a form you can fill out to submit your link. Just give it a title, paste the link in the URL field, and specify a subreddit for your link.

You can also click the "text" tab at the top if you are only submitting text (such as for an IAmA or TIL post).

Keep in mind that some subreddits have very specific rules about what type of content may be posted to the subreddit. For example, the "funny" subreddit specifies that political humor should be posted in the /r/politicalhumor subreddit instead.

Users and Karma in Reddit

You can view other Reddit users and their actions on the site (such as comments they've made or links they've submitted) by clicking on their name next to the comment or link. If you notice that there is a certain user who consistently shares links or makes worth-while comments, you may follow that user by visiting his profile and clicking the "+ friends" button.

You might also notice users' "Karma". Karma on Reddit is a measure of the overall votes that a certain user has received for sharing links or making popular comments. You can hold as much or as little stock in Reddit's Karma system as you like—it does not affect your overall interaction with the website, but instead acts as a summary measurement of what you've contributed to the Reddit community. Of course, it's easy to get a bit competitive!

Rules and Reddiquette

Reddit is a very open platform, but they do list a few rules to abide by if you wish to participate:

- *Don't spam.*
- *Don't engage in vote cheating or manipulation.*
- *Don't post personal information.*
- *No child pornography or sexually suggestive content featuring minors.*
- *Don't break the site or do anything that interferes with normal use of the site.*
  -taken from www.reddit.com/rules

When posting or commenting, you should do your best to practice good Reddiquette, "an informal expression of Reddit's community values as written by the community itself." You can view the full list of Reddit do's and dont's by clicking the "Reddiquette" link at the bottom of each page or visiting www.reddit.com/ help/reddiquette.

Some examples of proper Reddiquette are using good grammar, finding the original source of the content you share, and adding a NSFW (Not Suitable For Work) tag to any share or comment that might contain nudity or violence. You should also avoid insulting other users or commenting in ways that do not add to the overall discussion.

Preferences

At the top of the page, you can find a link to your preferences. Many of the default settings will be good enough for the beginning user at first, but over time you might find some of these tweaks helpful. As you become more familiar with using Reddit, you might want to change the number of links shown at once to more than 25, or increase (or decrease) the number of comments shown in the comment view. One very useful preference is found under "clicking options"—"open links in a new window" can save you from having to always use the back button to navigate back to Reddit when you have finished viewing a link.

Getting more information

Reddit has a fantastic help section, particularly the Frequently Asked Questions page. To access this page, or any other help page, simply use the link at the bottom of every page in the Help section.

The frequently asked questions page will explain a bit more in-depth how the site works and might clear up some confusing traits of Reddit (for example the host of acronyms used on the site).

ABOUT THE AUTHOR

Scott La Counte, writing under the name Scott Douglas, has sold over 100,000 books. He is also the co-creator of the bestselling Shakespeare iOS and Android app "SwipeSpeare" and co-founder of two publishing companies: Golgotha Press and Minute Help Press—which have sold several million books. In 2016, he co-created BuzzTrace—online software to help authors discover their audience.

CPSIA information can be obtained
at www.ICGtesting.com
Printed in the USA
LVOW10s1035160417
531004LV00010B/597/P